CW01667796

Old English Sheepdog

Training Book for Old English Sheepdogs

By

BoneUP

DOG Training

Dog Care, Dog Behavior, Hand Cues Too!

Are You Ready to Bone Up?

Easy Training * Fast Results

Old English Sheepdog

boneUP DOG Training

By Karen Douglas Kane

The Author and Trainer

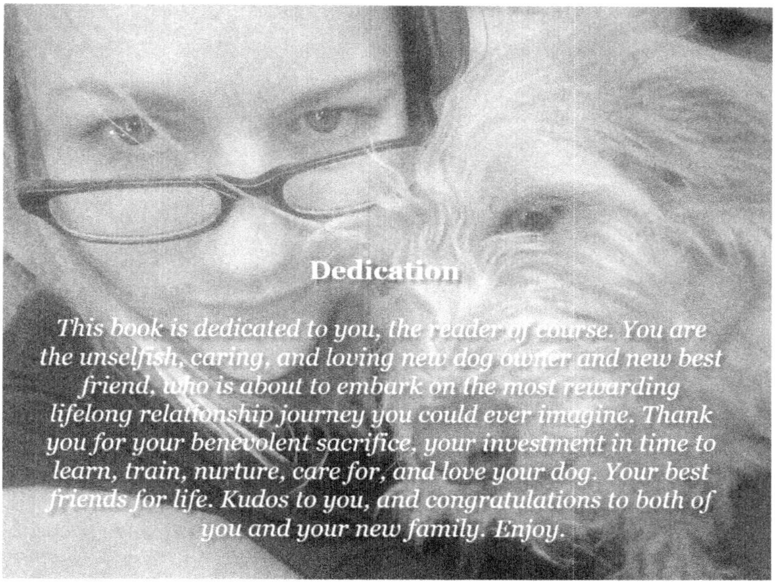

Author, Dog Trainer, Karen Douglas Kane

I'm Ready, Thank You.

Photo Attr: Squigman, Public domain, via Wikimedia Commons

Let's Bone Up!

Table of Contents

Introduction....................1
OLD ENGLISH SHEEPDOG Bio.................... 4
Old English Sheepdog Fun Facts.................... 9
Socializing Your Old English Sheepdog....................10
Attitude (Yours)....................10
Fear Imprinting Phases....................16
Taking Care of Your Old English Sheepdog....................19
Exercising Your Old English Sheepdog.................... 26
Grooming: 27
Anal Sacs.................... 32
Shots for your Old English Sheepdog.................... 32
Health Problems.................... 34
Mentally Stimulating Activities.................... 34
The Dog Den.................... 36
Why Crate Training is Important.................... 36
How to Begin Crate Training.................... 36
Picking the Perfect Crate for your Old English Sheepdog.................... 38
Where to Place your Dog Crate.................... 39
Furnishing the Crate.................... 39
Bad Dog!....................41
Proper Discipline.................... 42
No Jumping.................... 44

No Chewing 45
No Digging... 46
No Barking..47
No Nipping 50
No Chasing 51
No Running Away 53
No Aggression 53
Clicker Training 56
Things to Consider 56
How the Clicker Works 57
How to Perform Clicker Training 58
Good Boy! 61
When to Start Training 61
Positive Reinforcement Not Punishment 62
Consistency is Key 63
Secrets of Potty Training................................ 64
Secrets to Leash Training Your Old English Sheepdog... 65
Basic Dog Commands.. 68
Sit.. 68
Down.. 69
Stay 69
Fetch 70
Drop It 70

Leave It 71
Understanding Doggy Language 73
Posture 73
Tail 76
Face 76
Barking 77
Growling 77
Whimpering 78
Howling 78
Hand Cues – Pretty Handy! 79
"Sit" Hand Cue 79
"Stay" Hand Cue 80
"Down" Hand Cue 81
"Leave it" Hand Cue 82
"Quiet" Hand Cue 83
"Come" Hand Cue 84
"Good Boy" Hand Cue 85
Alpha Dog 87
How do You Become the Alpha? 88
Thank You! 93
Free - Gift for You 94

Introduction

Hi there. Did you just get a new Old English Sheepdog? These pups are sometimes called "Sheepdogs" due to the length of their name. Whether a puppy or adult dog, you just got a new best friend who will warm and enrich your life for at least a decade to come. You made a great choice by letting a Hound into your life. Your new dog will never betray your secrets or leave you for someone else. He will stay by your side, loving you for a lifetime to come, be a great addition to your family, and he'll provide all your loved ones with years of joy. Your Old English Sheepdog can perform work for you, and guard your safety, your home, and all your possessions you hold dear to you. You will get hours of amusement, and maybe even some hilariously cute, and fun filled viral Internet videos with your best friend. The benefits of dog ownership are too many to be counted.

Your relationship with your dog must be a positive one. No one wants a wild dog who cannot be controlled, or worse, an aggressive and mean dog who is no fun to be around. Establishing a good relationship with your dog from the minute you bring him home will ensure that the years to come are good years.

Starting a good relationship with your dog involves plenty of training. Don't let this overwhelm you. *You Got This!* If you start training *your Old English Sheepdog* right away and use the methods outlined in this book, you will have no problem raising a nice and obedient Old English Sheepdog who respects you and will do what you want, when you want, on your command. Dogs are naturally loyal and loving creatures who want to please their best friend and master - *you*. You must teach him how to please. Teach him that your word is law and that he needs to mind you.

In this guide, you will learn everything you need to know about training your dog. You will learn how to discipline him properly to end problem behaviors before they would get out of hand. You will also learn how to have your dog obey basic commands and even perform some cool tricks. This book covers everything from leash training, potty training and hand cues, and verbal commands.

Your relationship with your Old English Sheepdog is not just about training. It is also about bonding. You want to bond with your dog the right way. In the following chapters, you will learn how to become the alpha, so that your dog minds you. At the same time, you will learn how to be able to love him and play with him. Your Old English Sheepdog craves your commanding alpha presence and voice. But being alpha does not mean that you can't have loads of fun with your pet. It also does not mean that you must act or be mean or aggressive. Firmness is what you are going for, not meanness.

You also need to know how to care for your Old English Sheepdog. Your new dog needs proper nutrition, grooming and veterinarian care to stay healthy. You can prevent or mitigate health problems down the road by feeding your dog properly, taking him to the vet every year for check-ups, getting his shots and wormers on time, exercising him mentally, physically, and grooming him correctly. Everything you need to know about caring for dogs is covered in Chapter 2, as well as on my website here at NewDogTimes.com

When you get your dog, like most of we humans, you probably want a best friend. This best friendship is only possible if you act now and teach your dog to respect and obey you. It is also crucial that you form a friendship with your dog where he looks up to you as his master but also trusts you and wants to be around you. Being gentle but firm with your dog from *day one* is key to forming that lasting and trusting loyalty that will never die.

Therefore, if you are ready to start turning your new Old English Sheepdog into a good boy he wants to be now, read on. This Old English Sheepdog training book will help you form a best friendship with a loving, loyal dog who craves your attention and jumps at your command. You will complete this guide knowing how to care for your friend, how to stop bad behavior, and how to teach and reward good behavior. You will also learn other cool stuff, such as breed-specific facts and keys to understanding your dog's communication since he cannot speak.

Chapter 1

OLD ENGLISH SHEEPDOG Bio

You got yourself an Old English Sheepdog. That is wonderful, because Old English Sheepdog are eager to train, loyal dogs. You will love getting to know and train your new best friend. First however, you should learn a few things about the breed to understand how to train your Old English Sheepdog in the ideal way.

Bio

Old English Sheepdog are just one of several breeds that fall under the AKC Herding Group. Dogs that fall under the Herding Group can be all breeds and sizes but share common skill of herding animals. These Old English Sheepdog are full of energy and don't tolerate boredom well. They will require stimulation, exercise, and attention. These pups are recognized as an ideal family pets due to their spirited and happy demeanor. These pups may be possessive of their toys and food but are generally an excellent pet. If you are introducing your Old English Sheepdog into a double dog household, make sure you take the introduction slowly and don't force either animal to befriend the other.

Old English Sheepdog are large sized pups. They have a distinct dark brown or black hind area and largely white or beige coat. They typically have a solid brown or black head, with a lighter brown shade around the muzzle. They have a deep chest and a body that is tall off the ground. In a sense, they sort of have the clunky build of a bear. Their long and wavy fur is voluminous and fluffs away from their body Their stare is determined, and their ears lay relaxed at the side of their head. They have a coat that is typically long and wavy and will need moderate grooming .It is important to note that while there is variety in the appearance of these pups, the most common coat color is white with spots. Old English Sheepdog are an ideal weight if you're looking for a large sized dog; they weigh on average between 60 and 100 pounds and full of muscle Their height typically ranges from 21 to 22 inches.

Old English Sheepdog are incredibly loyal companions. They are affectionate, active, and friendly to those that they love. It may take some effort for your Old English Sheepdog to warm up, as they are typically reserved around strangers. Generally, they are great around children and other dogs when socialized properly. Because they are incredibly intelligent, they are fairly easy to train. It should not be difficult to house train this breed. They are eager to be around people and can actually become quite miserable if left alone for too long. But exercise caution as these pups are easily excitable and can accidentally knock over children with their exuberant behavior. These pups are frequently surrendered due to various reasons such as running away or causing too much damage (likely due to their energy level). It is important to remember that this breed was originally used to hunt small prey, so it is important to be cautious around other small pets

History

The Old English Sheepdog sounds like a generic sheep dog, but despite their name, they typically weren't used to herd sheep. In fact, these guys were used to as drover dogs, necessary to push cattle along. Bred in British, just like the Bulldog and Collie. They were used for sheep herding. This breed was created by mixing Bearded Collie from the British Isles and Russian Ovtcharka.

They were bred to be agile and smart for the use of herding. The name comes from the sheepdog's elegant coat, which is fluffy and light, much like a sheep. Farmers would often dock the dog's tail to keep animals from biting it. Because of this, Old English Sheepdogs got the nickname Bobtail.

Old English Sheepdogs were recognized by the AKC in 1888. In addition to being excellent companion pets, Old English Sheepdogs consistently wont various AKC competition.

Characteristics

An Old English Sheepdog has long wavy hair that requires moderate brushing and checking for ticks and fleas, especially if they will be out in the woods. Their double coat is quite frizzy and easily snags particles from the environment (think leaves, grass and small twigs) but be cautious just in case

These dogs live roughly 10 to 12 years and are prone to some health problems, specifically hip dysplasia.

Surprisingly, this is one of the only genetic disorders associated with the breed.

Hip dysplasia occurs when the hip joint damaged. This damage is due to normal lifestyle wear and tear, and can lead to limping and lameness. Supplements of the nutrient Glucosamine (which can be bought at your local grocery store) has been proven to help prevent and treat hip dysplasia. However, for more advanced cases, the vet may prescribe alternative forms of medicine. Be sure to ask your veterinarian what you can do to prevent breed specific issues.

It is important that you get your dog from a trusted breeder, who has completed the necessary genetic testing.

Generally, you should feed your Old English Sheepdog one to two cups per day depending on the dog's weight. If you desire to feed your dog some wet canned food too, begin by substituting half a cup of wet food per day to the dry food diet.

What to Expect when Training a Old English Sheepdog

Old English Sheepdog are quite easy to train. You simply must assert yourself as the alpha dog. Immediately start disciplining and training your puppy to show him who is boss. Begin from the car ride home. He will quickly accept you as the leader and work hard to please you. Old English Sheepdog typically do not need lots of harsh discipline. Once you show him that a behavior is undesirable, he will learn not to do it.

You want to socialize your Old English Sheepdog to ensure that he grows up into a well-rounded and normal dog. You also want to keep him active. A common problem that people encounter with these dogs is boredom. A bored Old English Sheepdog will start tearing up furniture and digging holes. Keep him active with hard play and running. Be sure to exercise him before training to ensure that he is more attentive.

Housebreaking your Old English Sheepdog is a fairly-easy task. Just stay on top of it. Don't put it off, but instead start working with him the minute that you bring him home. It is recommended to use 'respect training' to get your Old English Sheepdog to listen to you. If you don't establish yourself as the head of the pack and the alpha, he will not listen. Train him from a position of authority, where he is expected to do what you want simply because you say so.

You should also work to train your Old English Sheepdog using words. Old English Sheepdog are fast learners and will quickly develop an understanding of commands. If you establish respect, your dog will be more than happy to obey you once you utter a command. You'll get a kick out of how fast your Old English Sheepdog dog learns.

Enjoy your Old English Sheepdog dog!

Chapter 2

Old English Sheepdog Fun Facts

- Old English Sheepdog are named after the area in which they hail, England.

- The Old English Sheepdog are nicknamed "Bobtails" due to their short-docked tail.

- Old English Sheepdog make great all-around farm dogs.

- Due to the nature of the breed, these pups have endless energy.

- Old English Sheepdog are resilient to most weather conditions and thrive year-round.

- Due to their energy level and size, it is important to professionally train your Hound, and provide mental activities.

- Old English Sheepdogs are not banned under the Dangerous Dog Act.

- The Old English Sheepdog is featured in Disney's Little Mermaid.

Chapter 3

Socializing Your Old English Sheepdog

How to Condition Your Old English Sheepdog to Get Along with Everyone

Socializing your Old English Sheepdog puppy from an early age is essential. Do you know why? Because a dog who is socialized well is not aggressive toward other dogs or people. He knows that other dogs and people exist and are not necessarily threats to his territory. A dog who is not socialized, on the other hand, feels as if the world is his own and he's the only dog allowed to be in it. He gets angry and threatened when other dogs or people show up. So as soon as you bring your puppy home, you need to start socializing him. Get him used to having other people and dogs in his life.

Attitude (Yours)

Your attitude is very transparent to your Old English Sheepdog. He can read you like a book. When you are upset with him, he can sense it. He can also sense when you are in a bad mood, and he won't understand that your bad mood has nothing to do with him.

Therefore, during the process of socialization, you must take care to have a good attitude. Your puppy will bond better when he gets good vibes from you. Always be patient, gentle, encouraging, and loving.

Show more pride and happiness than anger or frustration. If you do get frustrated, step aside for a minute, take a deep breath, and try a new activity with your puppy, then return once you feel calm, cool and collected. Positivity is going to be your key to success when training your Old English Sheepdog. Don't keep pushing your dog and getting mad or you will ruin the training experience and overall results for both of you.

A huge part of socializing your dog is conditioning him to become the type of dog that you want him to be when he is an adult. The dog he grows into is largely shaped during the first eight months of his life. Therefore, you want to do the most work during this period and focus on your end goal. (The earlier the better is the rule of thumb when training) So have a plan, and stick to it, be consistent, *know* what you expect of him and make it clear. Really get happy and excited when he does what you want and reward him handsomely for desirable behavior. When you follow these principals, you can be amazed at how great you are at training your new Old English Sheepdog.

Another huge part of socializing is forging the special bond that you want to share with your Old English Sheepdog for the rest of his life. You must do this by teaching him that you are the master. But you also want to teach him that you love him and that you two are best friends. If you take the right approach outlined in this training guide and treat your dog like a best friend from the beginning, he will become the most loyal and loving friend that you have ever had. Approach socializing with the attitude that you want to be friends with this dog but be sure to also show that you are the dominant friend and the pack leader. Be gentle but firm. Provide direction without being mean or aggressive. Firmness is always better than aggression when socializing a Old English Sheepdog puppy.

When and How to Socialize Your Puppy

Your Old English Sheepdog puppy already begins the socialization process when he is just three weeks old. Until twelve weeks, he socializes with his litter mates and learns to play with them as well as his mother.

Of course, you cannot just expect a puppy to learn how to be a good dog from his litter mates and his mom. You must take care to expose him to humans and get used to human contact from seven to twelve weeks of age if you have him at this early stage. Simply because this is the most impressionable time of a puppy's life and it really shapes your dog as he matures. And if your Old English Sheepdog is a bit older when you invite him in your life, don't worry about your effectiveness in training him. You will just need to spend a bit more time on it. From the minute you get your Old English Sheepdog puppy, you need to start handling him properly as the alpha. Move his body, pet him, and play with him. Get him used to being handled by humans. He will learn that you mean no harm and that he is safe with humans.

Expose your puppy to multiple environments. Take him outside, on walks, go to the park where there is plenty of grass, concrete walks, social structures, plants, other dogs, and lots of people, walking playing and picnicking. Take him to the beach, a lake, a stream, a pond or your local pool. You get the gist here. Have fun with it, get creative and introduce him to several different landscapes, from natural settings to neighborhoods, and cities. Put him on different textured blankets, flooring, rooms, hallways and stairways too. Traffic, planes, trains and automobiles provide a good variation of fast and loud sights and sounds while making sure while even if holding your puppy in your arms, he is secured with a leash always.

This teaches him that's its okay to be curious rather than afraid of many different and new things. A worldly dog is a good dog. When you have friends over, let them play with your Old English Sheepdog puppy so that he gets used to them and learns to like different people. You don't want him to get overly attached to you so that he distrusts other people.

Spend a lot of time playing with your puppy, because it will bond the two of you tightly. It also teaches him what is acceptable and what is not when it comes to interacting with you, and others. It teaches him that you are a good, trustworthy master who loves him and being with you entails happy, fun times. Also. It's a good idea to find and create lots of mentally stimulating and physical activities to keep him engaged and active.

Note: It's imperative to give your Old English Sheepdog some alone time. This teaches him not to be anxious when you are not available to play with him. Put him in a crate by himself for an hour or two a few times a day to let him sleep. Let him outside to play by himself or with other dogs, but not you.

Don't be afraid to discipline your Old English Sheepdog to prevent bad habits early on. If he nips you in play, tell him "No" firmly. Tell him "No" when he messes in the house, even if he is too young to understand potty training. Don't let your dog get away with chewing and tearing up your stuff. Of course, he will because he's a puppy, but if you teach him early on what is *allowed* and what is not, he will grow into a more obedient dog and you will have less corrective action further down the road. You can do this by supplementing his chewing a couch with chewing a tantalizing Nyla bone instead. Unless you want to go furniture shopping on a bi weekly basis, a chew toy can be a spectacular alternative for your puppy and your wallet.

Stopping the bad behavior and replacing it with a good one will show him that you are the boss and he needs to mind you. Believe it or not, he craves this from you. Let him know which behaviors are acceptable and which are not starting right away. Be firm, not cruel. Avoid physical punishment and yelling, as these actions can traumatize your puppy for a lifetime. You don't wish him to cower, but to respect you with pride in his paws. All it takes is a firm 'No' and redirection to another activity to change a behavior while disciplining your pup.

After twelve weeks, it's time to start lightly training your Old English Sheepdog puppy. Of course, we cover that in depth throughout this dog training book. By twelve weeks, you can begin leash training and other forms of training to make your Old English Sheepdog obedient.

We'll cover this in more detail soon, and it's a natural need for the two of you, but you will want to work on potty training and leash training first.

Also introduce him to his crate and show him that the crate is a safe place where he can go for peace and quiet. Never use the crate as punishment, or you will make him grow up to hate the crate and avoid it at all costs. You will learn that your dog loves his crate because it's his private me-time-place, which for him, is also a feeling of being safe and secure.

A great idea is to enroll your Old English Sheepdog in a puppy class before he reaches three months of age. A puppy class lets him meet new dogs and people while learning basic obedience. They are fun for the dog and insightful for you as the owner. Be sure to vaccinate your puppy at least seven days prior to enrolling him. You don't want to lose your beloved pup to a disease like parvo, for example. Should you decide to take him to puppy school for advanced training, most puppy classes will not accept dogs without their shots.

By the time your Old English Sheepdog becomes six months of age, you need to begin serious training.

Meaning, at this age, you can successfully teach him things such as to sit, lie down, and roll over with little resistance and one hundred percent success. You will learn all about this in our upcoming basic commands chapter.

It's playtime. Set up play dates for your dog so that he learns to interact with others. Be sure to walk him and play with him to get him conditioned to the world around him. Expose him to a wide variety of people, dogs, and places to get him over fear and show him to accept the world as it is.

Socializing lasts for the Old English Sheepdog's entire life. You can't lock him in the house and never expose him to other dogs or people and expect him to be normal around them when he encounters them again. Socializing and training your Old English Sheepdog, is a life long journey. Small steps every day will go a long way.

Fear Imprinting Phases

Keep in mind that puppies go through two fear imprinting phases, one at eight to eleven weeks and another at six to fourteen months. During these two phases, your puppy is more likely to develop phobias. Any negative stimuli can leave a lasting impression on your dog, creating a fear that endures for the rest of his life. For example, your Old English Sheepdog might become afraid of all men if a man is abusive toward him during this phase. Or he might become afraid of kids if a kid is always pulling on his ears and tail.

To avoid creating fear in your dog, try to avoid exposing him to frightening things, like loud noises such as fireworks on the 4th of July, yelling in anger, or avoidable pain inflicting actions. Don't discipline him over zealously during these phases of his life, instead be gentle. Expose him to things like traffic, loud music, and other normal environmental stimuli by taking him for regular walks around town, in order to condition him to drop the fearful attitude and show him that most stimulus is harmless. The more you expose him to the real world around him, the less afraid he will be.

Of course, some dogs develop weird phobias. My dog was afraid of narrow stairwells for no discernible reason. It took a whole bag of treats to get over that one *(for both of us).* On the plus side, we did get plenty of exercise, so there's that.

For instance, your dog might become afraid of a balloon just because he hates the way it sounds when it rubs on surfaces. In such a case, I don't recommend popping it. That might just scare the *bajeebers* out of him *(all over your freshly waxed terra cotta floors.)*

When your puppy starts to develop a fear, try to work through it with him, and show him that everything is OK. Back to the balloon example, you can try holding balloons and bringing him up to them while encouraging him and telling him he's a good boy. Let him realize that the things he is afraid of really won't hurt him. Help him develop positive associations instead of negative ones.

If your puppy has a bad experience with a person, another dog, or any other animal, he may become timid. But this fear does not have to be permanent if you take care to correct it and recondition him. It's a good idea to expose him to nice and friendly, happy people, dogs and animals to show him that not everyone is the *Unabomber*. For example, if there is an untrained dog at your local dog park that attacks your Old English Sheepdog you will want to avoid that dog for obvious reasons. Expose him to other more socialized and playful dogs to help overcome his fear of other dogs. Overcoming fear is a crucial part of socializing your pup.

You may also want to expose him to different sides of yourself. You can wear a hat, shave your beard if you are an adult male, *and have-said-beard*. If you want to that is, besides, (I heard it grows back thicker). You can wear sun glasses, a dress or shorts, instead of slacks or jeans. You can change your hair style, use a different smelling aftershave, or shampoo too. He will notice these changes. If you continue to talk to him and let him know that everything is OK when you appear different, he will learn to accept that sometimes your appearance or scent changes. Then he won't be so nervous about change.

Read on to find out how to take care of your new best friend.

Chapter 4

Taking Care of Your Old English Sheepdog

Essential Care for Your New Old English Sheepdog

Learning how to care for your Old English Sheepdog starting as soon as he is a puppy really helps you to mitigate future health problems that he may have. Feeding, grooming, and exercising your Old English Sheepdog properly is essential for each phase of his life. You want to take him to the vet each month until four months, then once a month for all his shots until he's and adult, and there after once or twice a year. Oh, and be warned at visit, chances are he'll resist it. Keeping him mentally and physically active throughout his life, will help minimize problem behaviors.

Feeding

Canine nutrition is incredibly important for your dog's wellbeing. His nutritional needs will depend on his age, activity level, and breed. Be sure to pick the proper food for his wellbeing. Here is some advice on how to feed your dog, and what types of food you should choose.

Dry Food

When picking a dry food, ensure that the first ingredient is real meat. Don't pick up a brand that lists something like corn meal or wheat first. Also avoid words like by-product, animal, and 'meat parts', as these are terms for ground-up animal parts left over at the meat packing facilities. You want to find foods that contain real beef, real chicken, beef meal or chicken meal because there is more *actual meat* present in the food.

Select a dog food that offers a rich selection of vitamins and minerals.

There are dry foods specifically formulated for puppies, seniors, obese dogs, diabetic dogs, active dogs, large breeds, small breeds alike. Pick a type of dog food that matches what your Old English Sheepdog needs according to his health, weight and age.

Wet Food

A wet dog food diet can be useful for dogs who suffer from constipation. You can also feed wet food in combination with dry or raw food. Be careful with serving too much wet food, as it can cause diarrhea in your pup. Choose a wet food that contains primarily meat. Look for canned foods with lots of vitamins and minerals. Remember always, that your Old English Sheepdog has an entirely different digestive system than we humans. It is best to never feed your dog from your table, or while you are yourself snacking. This can be easily avoided by changing the natural begging behavioral habits while training your Old English Sheepdog. (*No begging = less guilt and more enjoyable snack times for you and your family or guests.)*

Raw Food

A raw food diet can be great for your Old English Sheepdog since it more closely mimics what he would eat on his own in the wild. However, you must take care to avoid feeding your dog contaminated food. A good rule of thumb is to avoid feeding your Old English Sheepdog anything you wouldn't eat. Stick to human standards and human foods safe for dogs in this scenario.

You can freeze meat and thaw it for your dog, or you can buy raw food mixes that are already prepared. The raw food needs to have more meat than any other ingredient. Dogs like veggies, though, so be sure to include things like peas and carrots. We will talk about what *not* to feed your dog in a few human minutes here.

How Much to Feed your Old English Sheepdog

How much you feed your dog depends on his stamina, age, activity level, and breed. You can gauge if you should feed your dog more based on whether you can feel his ribs. If his ribs don't stick out, you know that you are feeding enough. If his ribs become covered in fat, you need to cut back on food.

Here is a general guideline for feeding dry and wet food:

- 5 lbs.: half cup to three-quarters cup
- 10 lbs.: three-quarters cup to one cup
- 20 lbs.: one and a quarter cups to one and three-quarters cups
- 40 lbs.: two and a quarter cups to three cups

- 60 lbs.: three to four cups
- 80 lbs.: three and two-third cups to five cups
- 100 lbs.: four and a quarter cups to six cups

Remember that this is just a rough guideline that you can adjust as needed. But keep in mind that the average Old English Sheepdog is about thirty to sixty-five pounds when fully grown, so you would want to feed him roughly two to four cups of food.

When to Feed Fido

You should not wean your puppy from his mom until he is about eight weeks old. To grow properly, he needs his mother's milk during the first eight weeks of his life. After eight weeks can you begin to feed him store bought dog food?

Puppies need to eat three to four times per day. Establish a consistent feeding schedule. Avoid feeding your puppy too close to bedtime, or he will have to go potty while you are trying to sleep. Unless of course, you enjoy waking up in the dead of night, tripping on a chew toy or three, and cleaning up poop. Then again, it's a free world, who am I to judge you? Am I right?

Regardless, split your puppy's daily feeding portions into thirds or fourths and feed him at regular times each day. This helps with optimal nutritional absorption, digestion, and overall healthy regulation. For puppies, be sure to feed him only puppy food to give him the nutrients he needs to grow into an adult dog. You can soak dry puppy food in hot water to make it easier for him to eat and digest.

As your Old English Sheepdog enters adulthood, you can cut down to feeding twice a day as you make the switch to adult dog food. Continue to feed by weight and feed at regular times. An overall consistent routine is beneficial for your dog's mental well-being and sense of calm. I recommend feeding at seven in the morning and then five at night. Adjust according to your own schedule. Some dogs are content eating from the same bowl of food all day, so one feeding is all that is necessary. Other dogs like to *wolf down* their food, especially if they feel competition from other dogs that you may have in the home, so be sure to feed these nutty-gluttons twice a day. Simply split the daily feeding portion in half and feed twice. You don't want to overfeed your dog even if he *wolfs* his food down and acts hungry for the rest of the day. *Don't let him con you.* When it comes to food in their minds, it's always *go-time.*

One big part of dog ownership is establishing that you are the alpha dog in the pack. We cover Alpha Status in our last chapter, for now, what this means is you get to eat first. It may seem trivial, but it's a big contributor to establishing your alpha. He must wait patiently until you finish your food and clear the table. Only then should you feed him. Doing this establishes your dominance and teaches your dog that he does not rule the roost. He may need to go into his crate during your meal times if he is too rowdy with the begging for table scraps. He may begin to choose this on his own, or you can train it. *Personally, I get a bit uncomfortable when my pet 'Peeve' begs for my scraps and licks his chops while drooling on my freshly washed Bermuda's.*

Switching Foods

To switch food brands, try this switching schedule:

- Day 1-2 Mix ¼ new with ¾ old foods
- Day 2-4 Mix ½ new with ½ old
- Day 5-6 Mix ¾ new with ¼ old
- Day 7 100% of the new dog food

When switching your puppy to adult food, you should start at about nine to twelve months for small breeds, twelve months for medium breeds, and and twelve to twenty-four months for large breeds. Use the switching schedule above to introduce your dog to the new adult food. Usually it is best to stick to the same brand of adult food as the puppy food that you fed *Fido*, but you can switch if you find a healthier brand.

Healthy Treats and Snacks

Here are some healthy human foods you can offer your dog in his diet or as treats:

- Oatmeal
- Yogurt

- Apples with the seeds removed
- Peanut butter
- Cheese
- Bananas
- Beef jerky or other jerkies
- Meat, cooked or raw after being properly frozen
- Berries
- Melons
- Green beans. Be careful, as this can act as a laxative for your dog.
- Peas
- Squash and pumpkin
- Brewer's yeast. Not baker's yeast, which can make your dog very sick.
- Carrots
- Eggs
- Salmon or other fish

Foods to avoid at all Costs

I have touched on this above, but it's important to devote a section to the following: You now know that dog's digestion systems are different from our-own. Some foods that we can eat with no problem can be toxic to dogs. Avoid feeding your dog the following:

- Onion or garlic

- Chocolate. Especially dark chocolate
- Grapes or raisins
- Macadamia nuts
- Fruit pits or seeds
- Soft bones such as from pork or poultry
- Potato peelings or green potatoes
- Rhubarb leaves
- Yeast dough or baker's yeast
- Human vitamins or medications
- Broccoli
- Caffeine
- Alcohol
- Mushrooms
- Persimmons
- Avocadoes
- Raw egg. Can give your dog salmonella poisoning
- Xylitol which can be found in foods such as brand-named peanut butters

Exercising Your Old English Sheepdog

Exercise is essential to your dog's health. Just like people, dogs need exercise to stay healthy. A sedentary dog is prone to obesity, muscle problems, diabetes, and heart problems as he gets older. On top of that, a lack of exercise can create a bored dog, which in turn can create an unruly dog. You want to keep your dog occupied with plenty of fun, free play outside and with exercise.

Dogs require anywhere from thirty minutes to two hours of physical activity a day. Old English Sheepdog dogs need at least two hours. You can provide some of this activity just by letting him run around in a yard. But some of this activity you need to be proactive about. Play fetch or Frisbee to get him running. Take him on walks. Go for hikes together. This physical activity has the added benefit of getting you out and moving too. *Just, saying.*

Grooming:

Brushing

You should brush your dog's coat at least four times a week. Daily brushing is ideal when a dog is shedding. Some dogs shed year-round and have thick, heavy coats prone to tangles. You should make sure to brush such dogs every day, or you will have Old English Sheepdog fur all over your furniture and clothes and hairballs stacking up in the corners. Keep in mind that Old English Sheepdog shed moderately, so you will need to keep on top of brushing. *I can assure you it's mutually therapeutic after a long day.*

Have your Old English Sheepdog standing on all fours or lying down comfortably. Fussier dogs may need to lay down so that you can straddle them. Use a slicker brush first. Then use a long-tooth under rake to get deeper into your dog's coat.

Provide trimming or get professional grooming as needed. Dogs with thicker coats will need more trimming and grooming, especially in the hotter months. It's a good idea to let their hair grow thicker during the colder months in your region.

Bathing

You may be tempted to bathe your new best friend often, that is, if you're not one to enjoy the wretched stench of a dog gone wild. But keep in mind that his natural oils keep his skin and hair healthy. Too much washing can strip those oils away. Therefore, it is best to bathe your Old English Sheepdog only once a month.

Make sure to buy a quality dog shampoo such as Earth Bath Shampoo and a slip-resistant mat for those *"everyone gets wet shaky moments"*. Also have a hair dryer and three or four thick towels within easy reach. You want to wear clothes that you don't mind getting wet, and perhaps a little stinky too.

1. Lay down the slip-resistant mat nearby your tub for safety and comfortability.
2. Now gently ease your Old English Sheepdog into the bathtub. Dogs usually resist baths until they are used to the process. Be sure to make him feel relaxed by offering lots of praise and a treat.
3. Once your Old English Sheepdog is in the bathtub, you can start running the water. Before soaking your dog, test the water temperature with your fingers

carefully. Make sure that it is comfortable, lukewarm water.

4. Get your dog's entire body wet and begin rubbing in the shampoo to create a gentle lather. Don't use so much that you can't rinse it all out, but also don't use so little that you can't create a rich lather. Try your best to avoid his eyes and mouth. Rinse face often as necessary during bathing.

5. Trick: Bathe his head last. This is the part that he will shake and get shampoo all over you, the floor, the walls, and well, you get the picture.

6. Now rinse him thoroughly using lukewarm water. Gently work the shampoo out with your hands from top to bottom. Do this several times to get all the shampoo out so his natural oils can get busy keeping him healthy.

7. Now turn the water off and wrap him in a towel. Rub him down thoroughly. You can use a hair dryer after this to effectively dry his entire body. Caution: NEVER USE A HOT SETTING WHEN USING A BLOW DRYER! Place the setting on cool or warm and test it six inches from your bare skin on your inner side wrist. If you can hold it there indefinitely, your dog will feel comfortable while keeping him happy and from harm.

Nails (Claws)

Your Old English Sheepdog needs his nails to grip, scratch and dig. Yet, looking down at my own as I write this, there are nails and then, there are *nails!* Be sure to keep your dog's nails relatively short to prevent him from scratching you or injuring himself. If your dog's nails become resistant, you can have your local dog groomer or veterinarian do this for you at a nominal rate. Or you can do it yourself if your dog cooperates. You should buy a pair of special dog nail clippers.

1. Hold your dog between your legs if he is small, or if larger, have him stand.
2. Pick up each foot with your empty hand, so it bends naturally and comfortably. Trim each dog nail separately and delicately, taking your time on each. You never want to hit his quick, which is inside the dog's nail which contains blood vessels and sensitive nerve endings. Focus on the furthest end from the paw, the most translucent part of his nail that you can see through when you hold a light to his paw.
3. Dogs with white nails will have *obvious quicks*, which are pink and darker and thicker than the rest of his nail. Old English Sheepdog can have white nails but are more likely to have black or a combination of black and white.
4. In *black nails* that you can't see the quick, trim little pieces of the horn of his nail. Then inspect the nail to see if there is bleeding. Do it a bit at a time and be patient. You never want to hit the quick or you will cause your Old English Sheepdog pain and as a result, a bad association with nail trimming.
5. File the end to a smooth, round surface with a regular emery board.

6. Consider a smoothing oil, like coconut oil, to soften his paws. Use beeswax to heal cracks.

Your Old English Sheepdog's Teeth

Try to brush his teeth at least four times a week to prevent gum disease and other dental issues. You can buy a special dog toothbrush along with meat or poultry flavored toothpaste. Below is how to start brushing your dog's teeth.

1. Put a dab on your finger to let him smell and lick it to get him interested and somewhat comfortable.

2. Then try inserting your finger into his mouth and rubbing his gums gently and without too much force.
3. Soon he'll get used to this without too much resistance. When he lets you do this without a negative reaction, try using the dog tooth brush.
4. Use gentle but firm strokes to get his gums and all his teeth. It won't be perfect, but the idea is to get most of his dental surface area covered in the foam of the toothpaste.
5. There is no need to rinse. He will swallow the toothpaste without problems. However, encourage him to drink from his water bowl after a brushing.

Also, keep plenty of stimulating toys with nibs and dental chews around for your dog. These treats will keep him occupied mentally while also keeping his teeth clean and his gums strong and healthy.

Eyes

Check your dog's eyes regularly to make sure he has no irritation, bleeding, or swelling. Use a cotton ball dipped in warm water to clean away debris and eye boogers whenever you brush him.

Anal Sacs

My, Favorite section. We all know about the infamous anal sac. If not, you will become familiar soon enough. *Fact, It's one of the great wonders of dog ownership.* If your Old English Sheepdog dog smells bad or is frequently licking and scooting his bum on your carpets, you know that it's time to expunge the fluid in his anal sacs. Both female and male dogs have anal sacs that can become impacted at any age. The anal sacs are located directly beneath the skin around his anal muscles.

Ready to Expunge? Here's how:

1. Don a pair of plastic or rubber gloves.
2. Put your dog in a bathtub. This can get messy.
3. Rub gently upward and inward, pressing the glands toward his anus. *Like a teenager's zit on prom night.*
4. The fluid should ooze out of his anus. It should be a brown, strong-smelling oil. If nothing comes out, you may want to take him to the vet to investigate.

Shots for your Old English Sheepdog

Getting your Old English Sheepdog regular routine shots at the proper times will minimize his risk of developing a horrible disease like parvo, distemper, or rabies. It also makes your dog legal in your municipality and safe from those nasty dog catchers.

The regulations regarding shots varies by state. Generally, you want to bring your puppy in before three months of age (ideally six weeks) for the first round of rabies, distemper, parvo, adenovirus, parainfluenza, bordetella, lyme, canine influenza, and leptospirosis. Thereafter, for rabies, distemper, and parvo, you need to get yearly boosters for him. Most of these vaccines also require several rounds between six weeks and sixteen weeks of age. Get your dog on a regular schedule with your veterinarian. Ask your vet to send you reminders when it is time to get your dog his updated shots. *Or perhaps he can send a tweet to your dog.*

You also want to make sure to get your dog on heartworm pills. You should start administering pills to your Old English Sheepdog once a month, or per your vet's instructions, starting at six weeks old. Your vet will write you a prescription and you can set reminders on your phone to ensure that you give the pill as needed.

Wormers: Be sure to properly worm your dog. It is recommended to worm your puppy at two, four, six, eight, ten, and twelve weeks of age, then every month until they are six months old, and finally every three months for the rest of their lives. Regular wormers help prevent digestive problems and other health issues in dogs. Go to NewDogTimes.com to download a chart.

Health Problems

Health problems are common to all breeds of dogs. Most breeds have unique sets of common health problems that you must watch for. The best thing to do is to learn about health problems common to your puppy's breed. Then watch for signs and symptoms.

It is also essential to take your dog in for regular check-ups. Your dog may at first not favor a visit to his vet, but you can minimize his fear by taking him to the park before and after vet office visits. This will help him associate the vet with a positive and fun experience. In addition, reward him with a treat when at the vet's, after he cooperates. Being by his side as he gets shots and a check-up will go far in calming his nerves. *Preferably before your second cup of coffee.*

Mentally Stimulating Activities

We have already discussed how important it is to keep your Old English Sheepdog active and busy for both his physical and mental health. But physical activity is not all that your dog needs to be healthy and happy. Old English Sheepdog also need to keep their minds busy, or they can get bored and turn to bored-replacement activities like barking, chewing, and digging. You can prevent a lot of bad behaviors by providing your dog with mentally stimulating activities, like the following:

- Retrieval games. Add challenges by hiding toys or throwing them into hard-to-access places so that your dog must puzzle out how to get the toy.

- Obstacle courses. Turn your home, garage, or back yard into an obstacle course and make your dog overcome it by rewarding dog treats when accomplishing completion.
- A Kong full of peanut butter. He can spend hours trying to lick the peanut butter out. An occupied dog is a happy dog.
- Flyball. This will keep him active physically and mentally. You, probably just mentally :)
- Socialization and play with other dogs. He will invent his own games and feel very stimulated in the company of other dogs. Take him to the dog park or enroll him in puppy classes where he can play with other dogs.
- Herding livestock or Triebball. Triebball uses balls that mimic herd animals that dogs must manage.
- Tracking. Hide an object in the woods or a field and let your dog find it with his natural scent abilities.
- Herding trials or tests. These will let your Old English Sheepdog use his natural herding ability.
- Agility games. Set up an agility course in your yard and teach your dog obedience and tricks as you teach him to navigate the equipment.

Now read on to learn how to provide your dog with a nice den. In other words, crate training.

Chapter 5

The Dog Den

The Secrets of Crate Training Your Old English Sheepdog

Crate training your Old English Sheepdog is an important part of dog ownership. You will want to buy a nice dog crate for your Old English Sheepdog train him to use it in positive ways. The crate is a useful tool in keeping your dog calm, as well as training your dog. Plus, he'll love it.

Why Crate Training is Important

Dogs are inherently cave dwellers. They love having a den of their own. A dog crate can be a useful tool as well as a calming hideout for your dog. Your home is a great place for your dog to roam around in, but ideally you should provide a crate that he can call his own space.

The crate should be a positive place where your dog can relax. Therefore, the crate is never used for punishment. Don't use it for punishment, you will create a negative association to the crate and make your dog fear the crate. Instead he will search for a hiding place behind the furniture or otherwise in an unsafe place for his natural need for daily retreat.

How to Begin Crate Training

You can begin crate training your dog at any age. When you first get your Old English Sheepdog, give him a few days to explore your house and get used to his new surroundings. Then begin to introduce him to his new crate.

Start by encouraging your dog to enter the crate. Praise him when he goes in. Then lock the door and leave him in there for an hour at a time. Never leave him in there for more than four hours without a potty break. You can put toys or treats in the crate to help ensure that he feels it is a home atmosphere.

As your Old English Sheepdog becomes potty trained and learns not to tear up everything in sight, you can then leave the crate door open for him to use it as he pleases. He will probably go in there every now and again to take a nap or to rest for a while by himself, as well as to get away from other more dominating or active dogs, when he's not in the mood to socialize with them. When crate training, be sure to praise him when you see him going into the crate on his own to teach him that the crate is a good thing.

Always give your dog potty breaks. A Old English Sheepdog puppy needs to go at least every hour. Older dogs can hold it up to five hours comfortably. Also, be sure to remove soiled items from the crate, especially if your dog releases waste inside it in order that he does not turn it into his miniature porta-potty.

Once your Old English Sheepdog is fond of his crate, you can start to use it when you are gone. Leave the crate door unlocked once fully trained from bad habits. Let him use it freely. It can help to calm potential separation anxiety that he may suffer while you are away. If you do lock it, be sure not to leave him in there for too long, or adversely turn the dog crate into a punishment tool. If you do this, he will instead learn to not like the crate and soon being to resist going into it. This deprives him of his natural habit and need of it which and while you are gone, he will express as only he knows how to in the form of frustration, with barking, scratching, gnawing, nipping, howling, even whimpering, as well as other *naughty things* out of anxiety.

Picking the Perfect Crate for your Old English Sheepdog

Of course, the crate you choose needs to fit your dog. Buy a crate that will match your Old English Sheepdog's grown size. When fully grown, he should be able to stand up, turn around, and lie down in this crate comfortably. The crate will seem too big when a puppy is little. In such a case simply block off the extra space at the back of the crate. You can use a box or hang a towel to do so. This will help to prevent in-crate-pooping too. *Yes, I did just coin the phrase, in-crate-pooping. Use it free willingly. You have my blessings.*

A crate that is enclosed with only slats for your dog to see out of on the sides and the front is ideal for Old English Sheepdog. He'll want to observe his surroundings. This helps when things become noisy around him because he can see where the sounds come from.

The crate is not an isolation cell. However, you also want to make sure that the crate is not too open. It needs to be an enclosed den where he can have his privacy when needed. Open metal crates are not enclosed enough, cover it with a thick blanket, leaving narrow spaces on the sides that he can see out of.

Where to Place your Dog Crate

Place the crate close to where you spend the most time together while you are all awake in the house. Put it in a central area, against the wall. The idea is to keep your dog from feeling isolated and away from everything, while owning his own place in it too.

Furnishing the Crate

What you put in the crate is up to you. The crate should be a comfortable place where your dog can hang out as he wants, so be sure to place a pillow or some type of dog bed in it. You can also put toys and treats in the crate.

It's a good idea to put clean water in the crate. To avoid spillage and a mess, get a water bowl that clips onto the crate's door. You can also attach a food bowl if you will be crating your dog for a lengthy period while you are away.

When your dog is left alone, he will miss you no matter how much training he gets, or from whom. A great trick to reduce anxiety is to leave a piece of your unwashed clothing inside with him, such as a sock or shirt. If you want it back in good condition, you'll want to nip nipping and chewing in the bud first. Just saying.

In the next chapter will teach you how to humanely discipline your dog and find ways to prevent problem behaviors.

Chapter 6

Bad Dog!

End Problem Behavior Before It Starts.

You can expect problem behavior in your new untrained puppy. So, you will want to get on top of it from the get-go. Your new Old English Sheepdog puppy simply does not know any better at first but what is instinctive in him for survival. It's your responsibility to show him what is OK and what is not. If you don't discipline him properly, he will continue bad behaviors as he gets older and he won't understand why you are mad at him when he does them. Disciplining your dog without a reason is borderline abusive, if not too confusing and intimidating towards him.

If your Old English Sheepdog puppy suddenly becomes menacing when he is bigger, he will also have the idea in his beautiful mind that he is the alpha dog. To him, this means he does not have to obey you. It will not be his fault either, rather because you failed to establish Alpha Dog over him.

Let's say you didn't get a puppy, but instead you got an older, untrained dog from the shelter. He is filled with problem behaviors. Good on you to save him. Better on you is, that it is still not too late to establish dominance and teach him no.

Many pet owners make the mistake of being too easy or too hard on their dogs. Harsh physical discipline is usually never necessary. And spoiling your dog and ignoring problem behaviors is not a good idea.

You need to strike a balance by being gentle yet firm to establish harmony between him and you as the Alpha.

If you don't like something, you can say no. You have the ultimate say in what your dog can do and what he is not allowed to do. Don't be afraid to be the alpha dog and get bossy with him. He must mind you and that's that. *No barking back.*

All domesticated dog breeds crave your training, and the establishment of alpha. Some dogs are easier to train than others. Other dogs are more stubborn. Just be patient and persevere with your training. It is the only way to get your Old English Sheepdog to know what you want.

Also, be consistent. You won't succeed in breaking your puppy or older dog of problem behaviors if you sometimes discipline him and sometimes ignore it.

Avoid disciplining for things he did a long time ago. He won't remember. Also avoid praising him or giving him treats within ten minutes of disciplining him, or you will send conflicting messages. You may want to coddle him and comfort him if he is cowering and pouting after you say no because he is a cute little puppy, but don't give into this temptation. The key is to be very firm and consistent with your training always.

Always discourage bad behavior and reward good behavior. That's dog training in a nutshell.

Proper Discipline

There are a few forms of proper discipline that you should use on your Old English Sheepdog:

- **Dominance training:** When your puppy acts aggressive toward you or refuses to obey you, show him who is boss with dominance training. You don't have to be aggressive or mean to establish dominance. Here's how. Take hold of his scruff with one hand and his snout with the other. Stand over him and hold his head down. When he finally relaxes his body, or looks up at you, that means that he is submitting. Let go and praise him. (Your dog's scruff is the loose skin around his neck) Simply pull tightly to show dominance, without inflicting pain of any kind.

- **Saying No!** A loud and firm 'No!' can do wonders in training your Old English Sheepdog not to be a bad boy. When you are the alpha, your voice will impress your dog into obedience. He respects you by listening and craving your command.

- **Time out:** You can send your dog away by placing him in a time occasionally. This is a powerful and meaningful punishment, so don't abuse it. Find a boring place where it is quiet, such as the laundry room, porch or outside if there's nothing going on. When your dog does something, he is not allowed to be doing, simply tell him "*Time out*" and take him to the time-out spot. Tie your dog up on a shortened two-foot line or similar so long as he can lie down or sit comfortably and without the possibility of harming or worse choking. Leave him there alone for about five minutes. When he is finally calm, release him and tell him that he is a good boy.

- **Good Behavior:** Train your Old English Sheepdog good behaviors. We will cover this together in-depth, in upcoming sections in this chapter. But basically, you want to teach him good behaviors to replace bad behaviors as the goal. Reward all good behaviors. Yet when he commits a bad behavior, tell him "No" and command him to do the good behavior. A good example of this is when your dog barks. Teach him the command 'Quiet' and expect him to obey. Reward him when he does and discipline him when he doesn't. You want to show him how to act, so teaching good behaviors is a good way to do this.

No Jumping

Dogs tend to jump on people that they love as a form of greeting, especially you, his alpha master and provider of all things - him. They want to show you their love for you, they are happy you are back in sight again, and would really like to be petted. Jumping is their way of saying "Look at me!" While this may be cute in a small dog or a puppy, it can become troublesome when he gets to be over thirty pounds. It can disturb guests and make them uncomfortable, as well as possibly disrupt your family get-togethers in a negative way instead of a positive way with an obedient pup. Big breeds can scratch your legs, muddy your dress or slacks and if off balance when they greet you on their hind legs, make you fall over, or drop your groceries when you come through the door. It happens. Therefore, no matter how big your dog is, start to teach him that jumping on people is not polite behavior.

Start by saying "Whoa" when your dog jumps on you. Then leave the room. Reenter a few seconds later and repeat as necessary. He won't like that you leave when he jumps on you.

Of course, you can also tell him no when he jumps on other people and encourage guests and your family members to help you train him by having them say "Whoa" and leave the room too.

The minute your Old English Sheepdog stops jumping on you, reward him with plenty of warm and fuzzy attention. Bend down to his level to pet him. Show him that he doesn't need to demand attention by jumping on you because you will give it to him at his level when you are ready.

If your Old English Sheepdog refuses to stop jumping on people despite your efforts to train him, or if he engages in other attention seeking behaviors like the embarrassment of leg humping for instance, then you can use the time out method. Simply remove him from the room and tie him up for a few minutes when he jumps, humps, or does whatever you don't like. Only use this as a last resort, of course. Eventually when trained well, he should immediately obey your every command as the alpha dog you will become.

No Chewing

Chewing is a natural behavior that all dogs exhibit. Hence that brilliant Hollywood smile he gives you, with his forty-two long, sharp teeth. Chewing helps your dog keep his teeth healthy. Puppies who are teething, are especially prone to chewing on just about anything and everything within their jaws grasp.

It is important to give your Old English Sheepdog safe and healthy dog safe bones and chew toys to keep his mouth occupied, and his mind somewhat busy, when otherwise bored.

When you catch your dog chewing on say your new shoe, remove it at once, and tell him no. Replace it with a toy or bone. Say "Good boy."

If there is something that he won't leave alone, you can use a deterrent spray such as Grannies-Bitter-Apple or citronella to make it unappealing to him. He won't want to chew on it if it tastes horrible.

No Digging

A lot of dogs dig. Some dogs, such as Old English Sheepdog, do this because they are bred specifically to dig for prey. Other breeds, such as Malamutes and huskies, and other breeds do this to create a cool burrow where they can lie down and cool off. Yet others do it out of boredom. Soft dirt and sand hold a special appeal to dogs that can be difficult to break.

To prevent digging, you want to teach your Old English Sheepdog only to dig in certain places. If possible, create a special digging spot for him where you don't mind if he digs. Bury toys or bones in the dirt and let him dig for them. Most dogs love this activity.

When your Old English Sheepdog dog digs in other areas that are not OK, tell him "No" as you bury the spot in front of him. You can also fill a can with coins, bottle caps, or other junk. Hide and watch your dog. The minute he begins to dig, hit that can, startling him. Soon, he will create an association between digging and the unpleasant sound of the shake can, so he won't be as inclined to dig.

No Barking

The key to teaching your dog not to bark is prevention. You want to teach him not to bark his cute, furry little head off the minute anything happens, the minute he gets excited to see you, or becomes afraid or curious of a distant noise or knock at the door. When he is bored or frustrated, teach him to redirect his mind and busy himself with some other activity we discussed above, instead of just standing there barking at nothing, for no appropriate reason, and driving you and your neighbors crazy.

You know dogs bark naturally. It is his response to a variety of things. When he barks, he may be alerting you to potential danger. He may be warning other animals or dogs to stay away. He may bark to mark his territory or to greet you and express his excitement about going to play. Or he may be bored, and barking seems like something fun to do to pass the time. My dog will bark at me to wake me up if I'm sleeping too long (according to him). It's a clever thing dogs do with what they have, when they want to. I allow this because it's rare that this occurs, yet I find myself pleasantly entertained that he actually-thinks to bark me awake.

Fortunately, when abnormal barking is the problem behavior, it is easy enough to correct.

Prevention at Home Using a Clicker

The first step in teaching no barking is to teach your Old English Sheepdog to be quiet. The 'Quiet' command is a good way to prevent barking when you are at home. The minute he starts to bark, tell him "Quiet". Place a treat before his nose. When he goes quiet to sniff it, click your clicker and offer him the treat as a reward. Repeat and reward him for every few seconds that he is quiet. He will learn that being quiet means treats. Be sure to reward him whenever he is quiet in the future after some sort of trigger presents itself. He will soon learn to obey 'Quiet' and to stay quiet. And eventually the habit to be quiet will take precedence over barking.

If he refuses to listen to your 'Quiet' command, you need to take some proactive action to stop him from barking. Try blocking the stimulus that is upsetting him. Also use the *time-out* approach to take him out of the stimulus for a while and teach him that barking equals being tied up alone where he cannot observe and explore everything that is going on.

Prevention Away from Home

When you are away from home and you didn't bring Fido with you, you obviously cannot click and reward your dog as he is quiet. You want to take some steps to prevent his barking when you are not around.

First, try to remove as much stimuli as possible. If your Old English Sheepdog loves to bark at the mailman for instance, you should close the curtains so that he can't see the street.

Use a citronella spray collar as a humane way to condition him to associate barking with the unpleasant smell of citronella, which dogs hate. This collar will be triggered to spray him when he barks. He will learn to be quiet very quickly.

More Bark Prevention While Out and About Together

You can teach your Old English Sheepdog not to get all crazy with his barking when you are walking him or driving around in the car.

Start by teaching him the 'Watch me' command at home. Hold a treat up to your nose and say, "Watch me". When he looks at the treat, click and offer him the treat. Repeat this ten to fifteen times to help make it become a new positive habit. Then increase the wait time to two to three seconds in order that he looks at the treat and repeat this a dozen times. Finally, start to hold a *pretend treat* to your nose to teach him that this gesture means watch me. Keep increasing the times up to fifteen seconds.

Before you go out in public, start to practice this command outside of your house. Still keep him away from stimulus that will make him bark. Have him look at you for fifteen seconds before he receives a click and a treat.

Now, while out in public, try saying *"Watch me"* to redirect his attention from whatever he is barking at. Try holding the pretend treat to your nose to teach him that this gesture means to watch you. When he looks at you, offer him a treat. Soon, he will learn to look at you and stop barking when you are out and about together.

You can also try this command if your dog barks at a specific stimulus. When he barks, hold the pretend treat to your nose and use the 'Watch me' command until he stops barking. Teach him to redirect his attention from his barking catalyst each time.

If his barking still can't be controlled, it may be time to employ a citronella spray collar. You can put it on him when you take him outside or during times that he is likely to bark. Ideally, though, you will be able to train him to simply start barking when you pretend to hold a treat to your face. The gesture alone should be enough to get him to stop barking.

Prevention when your dog is Bored

The only way to stop *boredom barking* is to keep your Old English Sheepdog from being bored. You want to teach him to keep himself busy with toys, treats, and physical activity. Provide your Old English Sheepdog exercise for at least thirty minutes a day. Play mentally stimulating games with him. If he must be out in the yard, or in the house for extended periods of time without you, offer him things to keep him busy, like buried treats or a peanut butter-stuffed Kong.

No Nipping

Starting at an early age, you need to teach your Old English Sheepdog puppy that nipping your hands or your body and those of other's is NOT OK. You can do this by always playing with him while holding a chew toy. Show him that it is OK to bite the chew toy by not reacting when he does. If he nips your hand, say "Ouch!" and walk away. He will be disappointed that play time is over, and he will learn not to nip you if he wants to enjoy playing with you.

If walking away fails to teach him not to nip, then you need to use restraint to make him associate nipping with being put in a time out. Say "Time out" when he nips and take him to his time-out area. Tie him up on a 2-foot lead for five minutes and ignore him.

Teach your kids and other family members not to tolerate nipping. When they run away, he takes it as an invitation to give chase. Teach them to stand their ground or to simply say "Ouch!" and walk away without running and giggling or screaming.

Also, teach him to take food politely. Teach him the 'Polite' command. When you feed him, tell him to be polite. Reward him when he takes the food nicely. If he tries to nip, take the food away and don't feed it to him.

Keeping your Old English Sheepdog occupied is a good way to help him get over nipping. Nipping can be a big problem, especially if your Old English Sheepdog is in the teething phase of puppyhood. Give him lots of chew toys and bones to keep his mouth busy. Teach him that those toys are acceptable for him to chew on, but he can't chew on you or other people.

No Chasing

Your Old English Sheepdog will naturally desire to give chase to things they view as prey. To teach him to stop chasing prey of any kind, you can easily teach him the 'Watch me' command outlined in the section on barking to get him to pay attention to you instead of the prey he wants to chase down.

You can also teach him not to chase animals using a treat and a clicker. When he wants to give chase, command him to watch you or to sit. Use a treat to capture his attention. As he starts to look at you, click and reward him. Soon he will learn to stop chasing animals because he gets a reward for listening to you.

The time out method is good when your Old English Sheepdog refuses to listen. Remove him from the prey he wants to chase and tie him up for five minutes. Also do this if he gives chase despite you telling him no.

Be sure to train your dog to come to you when you call for him. It's especially important he obeys your come command particularly when the urge to give chase to something or someone. I'll cover teaching that command more in debt in the next chapter.

It's important to always keep your dog on a leash when outside. His instinct to chase is strong, and will not be easy instant, nor easy to break. You must protect your dog, other animals, and your neighbors with by keeping him on a proper leash outside your home.

Conditioning your dog around cats and other pets from an early age will teach him to treat these animals as friendlies, not prey or his next meal. Repeated exposure and interaction between him and other animals will help him learn to respect these animals.

No Running Away

A dog who runs away can get you into all kinds of trouble, or worse injury or death to your dog. You want to teach your Old English Sheepdog *not* to run away when he is bored, or when he sees something like a rabbit or deer.

Neutering or spaying your pet at an early age is a good way to help deter your pup from running away. Most dogs run away because they want to find a mate. If you choose not to neuter or spay your pet because you want to breed him or her, you might consider keeping him or her inside during heat. Of course, always walk your Old English Sheepdog on a leash, and keep him in a fenced yard where he can't escape by jumping over or digging under it. When dogs are in heat, they'll stop at nothing to find a hot date. Looks go out the window too.

Should your dog run away then come home on his own reward him when he comes back home. Show him that he is loved. Then he will want to stay home and always come home if after he runs off again. Prevent running away as the overall goal to protect your dog, and if any people and or their pets if he happens upon them when out in the wild beyond your fence.

No Aggression

Aggression is *never* OK. Your dog may be become aggressive for numerous reasons. The best way to deal with aggression is to make it clear it can never be directed toward you and others, nor tolerated in non-threatening circumstance.

The first step is to remain calm, not aggressive to him. Stand your ground. Never back down or you will teach your Old English Sheepdog he's the boss, not you. Display your dominance, show him not to be aggressive toward you.

When the doorbell rings or something else happens that makes your dog act overly aggressive, you should teach him to go to his crate. Start by ringing the doorbell (or presenting whatever trigger that makes him aggressive) and then luring him into his crate and giving him a treat. When inside your home, teach him to associate the clicker with going to his crate and then use the clicker whenever his trigger presents itself. Reward him for going into his crate with treats and praise. The crate is his safe place where he can relax, so it is helpful when he starts to get afraid or angry.

You may also need time outs if your Old English Sheepdog becomes aggressive toward other people. When he acts aggressive, tell him no and restrain him on a short lead, in his time-out area for five minutes, or until he calms down and stops barking and snarling. He will learn that being aggressive means that he must be alone, away from the action. He will want to stop being aggressive so that he can remain in the room with you and yours.

If your dog becomes aggressive because he is afraid, try to break him of this fear by giving him a treat and leading him away from what scares him. Expose him to his fears gently and from a safe distance. Provide lots of reassurance to him by speaking to him in a sweet, gentle voice. He will come to trust that you will always make everything OK and that his fears are unfounded.

Be sure to amply reward him when he is calm in the face of one of his aggression triggers. You want to teach him that being calm is the ideal behavior. Praise and treats are in order when he remains calm, not aggressive.

One trick that is great with puppies is to always handle his food and toys as you please. Teach him from a young age that you get to touch his stuff. He is not allowed to get all territorial when you touch what he considers his. He will learn to accept you meddling with his things and to not become aggressive with you.

In the next two chapters, we delve a bit more into encouraging good behaviors and training your dog. Read on to help your buddy become a good dog.

Chapter 7

Clicker Training

Learn the Power of the Clicker

In the following chapters I will be referencing the clicker quite often while going step by step and teaching you all training commands. This is because I strongly advocate the clicker and you should also. Clicker training is a very effective way to get into your dog's head and align his subconscious to act instinctively on command once a command is trained with it. The essence of clicker training is to use a dog clicker device that makes a clicking sound to teach your dog an association between the sound of the click, a command, and a reward if he follows the command. Dogs learn fast through conditioning, and the clicker really helps cement this conditioning.

Things to Consider

The first thing to understand is that the clicker is a teaching device. It is not something that you will always need to use. Once your dog learns to follow your commands, you can put the clicker away. You will not need to carry it on your person at all times during the entire course of your dog ownership. Unless you yourself enjoy the sound of a snappy clicker while on solo walks. To each their own.

The second thing to realize is that treats are not the only reward you can offer. They are very effective, especially when training your Old English Sheepdog initially. However, once he gets your commands down, you can more often reward his good behavior with love and praise, a toy, and only the occasional treat. Mix it up to keep him guessing and looking forward to what he might get if he obeys you.

Finally, dog treats don't need to be calorie-laden. Give your dog small things, like a tiny piece of jerky or a kernel of corn, or any number of brand name healthy and fortified doggie treats on the market. Here's why, because they are less than bite sized treats, although you treat him often enough, smaller treats will not tire him out, make him lazy or gain weight. Plus, they are easy to carry in your pocket, or you can purchase a dog treat pouch for a nominal price at amazon, or your local pet shop when on a walk with your dog. Keep these treats concealed. For instance, you are trying to teach your dog to sit, so you tell him the sit command. When he does it, you then produce the toy or treat hiding in your pocket and let him have it.

A good exercise is to stop your Old English Sheepdog during play and give him a command. Take his toy away and hold onto it. Use a command. When he does it, click and then give him the toy back.

How the Clicker Works

The clicker works using what's known in training your dog as shaping. Shaping is where you use progressive steps to teach your dog a desired command. You basically shape his mind by rewarding him each time that he performs a step as you desire. As well you will add more time to hold the command in each successive shaping. Eventually, your pup will learn to associate the clicking noise with a reward. He will learn that by doing something you ask, he will hear a click, and then he will get a reward. Eventually, the conditioning will become so strong that he will stop needing the clicker or the treat. He will just do what you command. *"Now, that's a Good Boy!"*

You may wonder why a clicker is better than saying "Good" or some other verbal cue. This is because the clicker is a unique sound that your dog cannot mistake for anything else. The human voice can vary in tone and sound at different times, and some commands sound alike in many of our English words. But the click never varies in volume or sound. It is consistent. And we love consistency in training your Old English Sheepdog.

How to Perform Clicker Training

Buy a clicker from amazon.com. Then use it whenever you teach your dog a new command, behavior or trick. Use a click when he gets the command right. Then follow it up with a reward.

Consistency is key. You want to use the clicker at the exact moment your dog does what you command. You can use it when he obeys a command you give, or when he does something on his own. Use your clicker during training until your dog has *listening to you* perfected.

Start by teaching your pup a command. When teaching him to stay, only click and reward when he is completely still. When teaching him to sit, you may need to push his body into a sitting position. Once he is sitting down, you click and reward. This teaches him exactly what behavior is desired when you make a command or give him a cue.

You can also teach him to associate responding to a certain stimulus with a desired behavior. For instance, staying quiet when the mailman arrives is something that you can teach him to do with the clicker. Click and reward him when he does not bark at the mailman.

Never offer a click or a reward when your Old English Sheepdog does not do the desired action. Doing this will only confuse him. You want to stay consistent. *As consistent as I use the word consistent even.* Teach him to only expect clicks and rewards when he does what you want.

If your dog is not responding to clicker training, then consider that you are doing something wrong. Maybe you are confusing him. Try working on teaching him the command or cue more. Read this again. Be clearer, more direct about it and eliminate distractions.

Maybe you are offering too many treats, so he is preoccupied with food and not listening to you. In this case, pause for a while. Twenty minutes or so, then return to training. Mix it up a bit and offer other rewards besides treats. On the other hand, maybe the reward you offer is not cutting it for him. I suggest you don't use sauerkraut, that's for a different type of dog you may find on the streets of New York.

Is he nipping and spitting, or gobbling them down as if each treat is the only one left in the dog world? Perhaps your Old English Sheepdog does not view it as worth the effort. In such a case, change the reward to something that he prefers. Switch out an unpopular toy with his favorite one or find treats that he really likes. For the life of me, why my dog likes one over the other, I'll never know, but I do know, all my dogs have their favorite. Your Old English Sheepdog will too. It's kind of cute learning their personality. You yourself are in for a big treat because of this.

Maybe you have only trained your dog at home. Now that you are out in public, he thinks the context is different. Work on graduating to new and different environments to get him to understand that commands or cues are the same no matter where he is.

Clicker training can come with some trial and error. Consider this a long-term partnership with your special buddy. Gauge what you do and how you do it based on his responses. Keep what works, dump what doesn't and replace it with what does. Command, Click, Treat.

Chapter 8

Good Boy!

Start Training Your Old English Sheepdog Early

Who's a good boy (or girl)? Your dog is, of course. Now you are about to learn the secrets to training your dog to do what you want. When you follow these steps, you can raise your Old English Sheepdog, a dog who is obedient and easy to discipline. He will do exactly what you want when you want, while loving every minute of it.

When to Start Training

Start training the minute your new Old English Sheepdog enters your life. It is ideal to start at eight weeks, when you wean a puppy from his mother. But you can really start at any age. While it is somewhat true that older dogs are a bit harder to train, this does not mean that they are impossible. Dog treats and lots of touch praising with repetition speak volumes to all ages in a dog's lifespan. You can accomplish a lot with an older dog.

The secret to training is to be a dominant figure that your dog respects. You must establish dominance by consistently disciplining your Old English Sheepdog and rigorously rewarding him when he does what you want. Don't tolerate behaviors you don't like and always reward ones you do like. Your dog will understand that you are a master who is responsible for his care, not a pushover who feeds him and does his bidding.

The other secret is to be reliably consistent always. Never give up. Every day is a new day to enforce your rules and teach new tricks or commands. Work on training every day to really cement it into his wonderful, happy, hard noggin. Expect your dog to obey, reward him for it, and take mild disciplinary action when he does not.

Positive Reinforcement Not Punishment

Never, ever punish your Old English Sheepdog for not doing what you want. Instead, teach him to not want to engage in bad behaviors by using the time out method or withdrawing play time, or a toy. Then teach what you do want by rewarding him well for obedience.

Punishment strains your relationship with your dog. It makes him fear you, not respect you. And he won't want to be your obedient little buddy if he fears you. Positive reinforcement, on the other hand, does motivate him to please you and makes him consider you his master. He will strive to please you if he knows that you will reward him for doing so.

The foundation of your training should be offering rewards for good behavior. When training your Old English Sheepdog use a dog training clicker, a treat, and plenty of praise. You will learn his preference early on. Teach him to associate obeying you with getting something good that he likes.

Make sure the reward means a lot to him so that it has more power. For instance, if your dog loves the dog park, you can reward him for good behavior by saying, "Let's go to the dog park." He will soon learn what that means, associate the reward, and he will start jumping around for joy. Treats and rewards serve as powerful motivators.

Above all, always show your Old English Sheepdog love. Praise him just for lying there or for being your friend. Dogs love hearing that they are good boys. Showing your Old English Sheepdog lots of love will create and cement an amazing loving bond between you two for life.

Consistency is Key

The other crucial part of your Old English Sheepdog training foundation is consistency. You want to always offer a consequence for each thing that your dog does. Bad behavior is never tolerated or condoned. Good behavior is always rewarded.

You need to be consistent with your commands. Pick a command, and process that works well, and stick to it. Switching up commands will confuse your dog because he will not know what you want.

Finally, a consistent schedule is ideal for your dog's sense of wellbeing and calm. You will have better luck training him if you train at consistent times, as well to feed, exercise, groom, and play at consistent times. He will get used to his schedule and will know what to expect. This helps him calm down so that he is more open to learning and being a good boy.

Secrets of Potty Training

House training should start immediately when you bring your Old English Sheepdog home. Don't wait or he will get stuck in bad habits. You can start potty training your Old English Sheepdog at any age, though of course it is ideal to start when your dog is a puppy, and moreover at the age and times suggested here in. The minute your furry friend enters your home, he needs to understand that this is where the pack lives. It is his private thrown. Give him a tour, prevent marking whilst touring his new surroundings and home.

One problem with puppies pooping and peeing is that they must pee every hour, and pooping happens more often in puppies than adult dogs. You will get messes in the house if you don't provide your pup with adequate pee breaks. On top of that, he does not yet understand that going inside is puppy dog no-no. Be sure to let him outside every hour and guide him to a specific place on your property to take care of his business. When he does his business outside, really praise him. Show him that peeing and pooping outside is a good behavior.

Some dogs also like to go inside the house to mark their territory. This may especially be a problem with male dogs who are not neutered or who were neutered late in life. The problem can also be compounded if you have other dogs present in the house. It is all about territory for dogs; they don't see it as ruining furniture, they see it as claiming that furniture for themselves. You can use a hormone spray to keep your dogs from wanting to pee on the furniture. While scolding your dog for doing his business inside is hardly effective, you can teach him commands like 'go outside' or 'no' when you spy him trying to lift his leg on your new couch. Remove him from the furniture and take him outside to his pre-designated place for relieving himself, whenever you catch him trying to mark his territory indoors.

Start by determining an elimination spot where your dog is welcome to go to the bathroom. Take him to this spot whenever you think he needs to go. Say "Potty time" to teach him that this is a command. Whenever he eliminates in his designated spot, really praise him. You can even use a clicker. Click when he goes and offer him a treat.

Take him out to his spot on a reliable schedule. For little puppies, this is forty-five minutes to an hour. For puppies four months and up, every four hours is OK. For adult dogs, you can go five hours if you must, though four hours is most recommended for your dog.

Try to teach him to tell you when he needs to go out. Not all dogs naturally whine at the door. Hang a little bell by your door and put some cheese or peanut butter on it. Every time he licks it and it rings, take him out to his designated potty spot. This forms the association in his mind between the bell ringing and going outside. When he needs to use the potty spot, he will know to ring the bell.

Secrets to Leash Training Your Old English Sheepdog

First you want to select a good leash. Use a head leash for big powerful dogs who want to walk you.

Front or head attachment leashes are also great choices. Try to select a leash with less than six feet of length. This prevents your dog from having the room to lunge out and potentially hurt himself if he sees something that he wants to chase.

Start in the back yard to get him used to being on a leash. Choose which side you want to walk him on and stay consistent with that side. *Usually on your left side but either side is fine. Both sides, even better.* As he walks beside you, reward him. Feed him a treat at your thigh level and use the word 'Heel' when he is approaching your side and before the treating When repeated enough times, he will learn to like staying by your thigh when you say the command word 'Heel' because this is where he knows he gets his treats.

Try going different paces. Make sure that you only reward your dog when he heels or walks right alongside you at your pace. If he lags or bounds ahead, don't reward him. Should he get distracted, say "Heel" and slap your thigh with the leash to get his attention. He will run to join you. Then reward him. Also increase the increments of time between rewards as he learns to walk alongside you obediently.

Now you can try taking your Old English Sheepdog out on the leash. Reward him when he keeps pace with you at your thigh. When he tries to pull and run ahead of you, simply turn the other way. Reward him with a click and treat when he falls into step beside you again. Also continue to teach him to "Heel" and guide him to walk alongside you at a pace matching yours. You are the leader and you want to establish that. He can only go where you want to go and walk as fast as you want to walk. This makes walking your dog a fun relaxing exercise for both of you and all you encounter on your merry way.

Chapter 9

Basic Dog Commands

There are many basic commands that you will want to teach your dog. Choose a quiet place to work with your dog for no longer than twenty minutes each time you train a command. Start training early. You can train on a leash at first for greater control, then move on to training without a leash once he starts to follow basic commands with little hesitation.

Sit

Sit is one of the first commands you should teach your Old English Sheepdog. When he sits on his own, tell him "Good sit" and click and treat. Then start to work with him by having him sit for you. The minute his hairy fanny touches the floor, click and treat. You may have to show him the movement by pushing his rump to the floor, but always click and treat the minute he sits down.

Come

A good dog comes when called. Start by telling your Old English Sheepdog to come while bribing him with a treat. He only gets the treat when he comes all the way to you. Now start to say "Come" in a variety of settings, particularly in situations where he is busy playing or is occupied with a toy. Only reward him when he comes to you. If he ignores you, repeat the command until he does. Eventually phase out treats and expect him to come to you when called, no matter what.

Down

Wait till your Old English Sheepdog is lying down naturally and click and treat him while telling him "Good lie down." Whenever you see your dog lying down, say "Down." Teach him what the command means before you use it in training. Once you are sure that he knows what 'Down' means, you can start to use this command and tell him to lie down. Click and treat whenever he lies down at your command.

Start taking him outside and practice this in a variety of different areas. Teach him that no matter where you tell him to lie down, he only gets a click and a treat if he complies. Gradually phase out treats and clicks over time as he gets comfortable lying down when you say so.

Stay

Teach stay by having your best friend sit. When he is sitting, wait a few seconds before you click and treat. Do this many times, extending the amount of time that your dog must sit there waiting. Then start by saying "Stay" and hold a flat palm to his face when he sits. Wait a few seconds, and then click and treat if he stays still. If he comes toward you, start over again without reward. He must stay sitting still to get his treat.

When your pup gets better at staying for up to a minute at a time, you can take it to the next level. Walk a few steps backward while telling him to "Stay". He will naturally want to get up and come to you. Direct him back to his spot and repeat the 'Stay' command with your hand signal. Keep walking away. Only treat your Old English Sheepdog when he sits still as long as you desire. Work your way up to two-minute increments of time between sitting and treating. Also start to practice things like telling him stay and then leaving his line of sight or even leaving the room. Reward him richly with praise and a treat when he stays. Or repeat when your Old English Sheepdog does not comply.

Fetch

Start by playing with a toy that your dog loves. When you throw it, tell him "Fetch." Click and reward only when he gets the item and brings it back to you. Soon, he will learn to do this for any item whenever you say "Fetch" because he expects a reward. Point at something and say "Fetch" to teach him to use this command in any situation. Always click and reward. Phase that out as your Old English Sheepdog becomes more proficient at fetching.

Drop It

When your Old English Sheepdog has something undesirable in his mouth, you can teach him to drop it the minute you tell him to do so. First, give him a toy that he likes. As he plays with it, hold a treat to his nose and say, "Drop it." He will drop the toy to get the treat. That's when you click and reward him.

Now start to conceal the treats. Practice this command ten times a day until he is willing to drop something for a treat that he cannot see. Eventually, you can phase out treats and he will drop something the minute you tell him to.

Leave It

The idea behind this command is that your dog will not eat or touch things that you don't want him to. For instance, you can get him to leave *roadkill* alone while on walks or stop focusing on that dead eyed rabbit staring right at him like dinner is served, or to stop chewing on something you don't want him to destroy.

First, have two treats in both hands. Let him sniff one of your hands. Next, he starts to lose interest because it's apparent he won't get the treat, click and treat him using the other hand.

Open your hand and show him the treat. Close your hand when he tries to get it. Repeat until he ignores this hand, knowing he won't get the treat. When he finally ignores it, it's time to click and treat with the other hand. You can also say "Leave it" when he pays attention to this hand to condition him to learn the command.

Take it to the next level by placing the treat in your open hand on the floor. He will run for it. Cover it with your hand and say, "Leave it." When he starts to ignore that hand covering the treat, click and reward him. Now uncover the treat and stand up. Tell him "Leave it" and reward him with a treat from the other hand if he does.

Start to practice this in a variety of settings. Do it while walking him, or while playing in the yard or neighborhood park. Tell him to leave toys he is playing with or treats that you drop on the floor.

Want to learn how to read your dog like a book? The next chapter is for you then. Reading your dog's body language is very helpful during training. It can help you see what your dog is feeling and how you can improve training.

Chapter 10

Understanding Doggy Language

The Key to Reading Your Dog's Body Language

Don't you wish that your Old English Sheepdog could talk to you? I do, too. Instead we need to learn his language to communicate our best with him. Your Old English Sheepdog actually-does communicate with you in a wealth of wonderful ways. Learning to read his barks and his body language can really help you understand him. When you understand him, you know what he needs. You can respond to his needs when you understand his unique speak and can become a much better provider and guardian for your mutual benefit. You and your Old English Sheepdog can grow a bond that is almost telepathic in nature. *It's uncanny really. I'm may just take my dog and human on the road. "(Scratch that)"*

You can also begin to pinpoint what is bothering him and why he might be acting a certain way. It can be helpful to know this so that you can mitigate whatever is bothering him to prevent problem behaviors. For example, if your dog is barking and acting aggressive because he is frightened, you can help him feel more at ease to end the aggression.

Posture

Your dog's posture says a lot about how he is feeling. If he is feeling submissive and giving himself up to you, he will roll over on his back, leaving his vulnerable tummy and genitals exposed. He may also pee himself a little bit as the ultimate show of submission. Reward your dog when he does this to show him that it is good that he respects your dominance. *Oh, and clean up that pee-pee please.*

Another sign of submission is if he bows his head down and pins his ears back. He may even tuck his head in, which is an instinctual motion to protect his head and throat from attack.

Be sure to take note if your dog has a fearful posture. A fearful dog posture involves cowering. He may twitch his ears back and forth as he stares ahead at whatever is striking fear in him. He may lay down, his paws straight ahead and his back legs curled under him, ready to run if he needs. His eyes will be wide open, showing the whites. The hair along his back will stand up on end. In addition, he may tuck his tail between his legs. Chances are, he will whine and even look to you for assistance. If he avoids your eyes that means that he is really scared.

A playful Old English Sheepdog will do a little jump in front of you and land with his front legs splayed out in front of him. He wags his tail vigorously and rolls his head around. You can't deny the excitement and joy in his face. He will do this with you or other dogs when he is in the mood to get a game going. Jumping up and down a bit in front of him will excite him more and probably make him take off running for the ball.

An aggressive posture shows that your dog is feeling threatened and wants to display his dominance. You should discipline him with dominance training when he assumes this posture with you or with anyone that you want him to respect. You should let him maintain this posture when he meets other dogs, as it allows him to establish his place in the canine pecking order. Dogs need to work out their hierarchy without human intervention. An aggressive dog stands straight up with his ears pinned back or sharply forward. It may even look like he is smiling, but his eyes are hard as he stares down his opponent. His hackles may be raised along his back. He may wag his tail once or twice in quick, precise motions. Everything about his body is tense, poised to attack. *For him, its go time.*

He will shoulder up to another dog or a person and try to appear bigger than he is if he is trying to intimidate. He will adopt this authority posture when vying with another dog for a toy, treat, or food. Don't ever let him adopt this posture with you.

A relaxed dog will appear relaxed. He may sleep curled into a ball, laying on his back with his legs sprawled out, or simply lying there watching you with his legs relaxed. You can tell that he is not relaxed if he keeps his legs tense and in a position that allows him to easily jump up.

A curious dog will tilt his head, raise his brow, wiggle his nose and twitch his ears. Don't worry, he's not about to cast a spell on you. He is a dog, not a witch. Also, he will be looking around. He may have his mouth open and pant, in order to help him smell odors better.

And he will wag his tail a few times. Perhaps seem antsy, and somewhat frustrated to know what's in your closed hand, as a for instance.

Tail

Usually, a wagging tail means that your Old English Sheepdog is feeling happy. He will wag his tail when he sees you or one of his friends at the dog park. He will wag when he eats something he really likes.

But watch out. Tail wagging can also indicate aggression. As noted, short, quick wags accompanied with an aggressive posture means your dog is upset.

He may also give tense wags while he is on the trail of a scent or busy working. When your dog solves complex mental puzzles, such as finding hidden toys or navigating obstacle courses, he may wag his tail as he concentrates. *Keeps him in the zone, if you will.*

On the other paws, when he tucks his tail between his legs, he is feeling fearful and possibly submissive.

Face

Your dog's facial expressions say a lot about what he is feeling, too. You may notice that you're Old English Sheepdog smiles a bit when he pulls his lips back, exposing his teeth. This joyous expression is just like when we smile. It means that he is feeling peaceful and happy, or excited. *Or perhaps he just farted, and you are about to get schooled by it.*

If he raises his upper lip and bares his fangs, accompanied with a low growl, then he is snarling at you. He means you harm. You better watch out. Use swift discipline if your dog ever snarls at you. He does not get to snarl at you, even if he thinks that you are about to take his food. As the master, you get to do what you want, and he can't do anything about it.

Some dogs always look sad. This does not necessarily mean that they are sad. They are probably just at peace and relaxed. A dog who pouts will whine and look at you with the most heartbreaking eyes. You should not give in and spoil him just because he looks at you like this.

Barking

Dogs bark for countless reasons. Your pup will bark as a greeting or to get your attention. He will bark at strangers, and at animals. He will also bark when he is bored, which can be controlled with a quality barking collar or clicker training. Short barks while he is jumping around indicate that he is excited. Barking in general means that he is excited, offering a warning, or bored and looking for attention.

Growling

Growling is an official sign of aggression. Your Old English Sheepdog never gets to growl at you. But he does get to growl at threatening strangers or other dogs to protect his family, Domain, and food.

Whining

Dogs whine to express what they want if they are not in pain, but instead asking for your help. If he is whining at the door, he wants to go outside. If he is whining while you eat, he wants some food. If he is just standing there whining, he wants to be included, to be petted or a toy to play with. Often you will be able to tell what he wants because he will whine while standing near or switching gaze by looking at something, then at you then swiftly back at the thing of interest. Whining is his way of getting you to pay attention to him and address his needs. Some are warranted, some are not. You decide which is which then train accordingly.

Whimpering

Whimpering always conveys fear. A dog will whimper when he feels threatened or scared. He may also whimper to get your attention when he wants something, or when he is in pain and wants your help.

Howling

If your dog howls, it may be because he hears other dogs howling, or a high-pitched noise like a siren or singing that reminds him of howling. He may also be feeling lonely and is raising his voice to hear if any other dogs are nearby. He may howl because he is feeling excited about a hunt or a scent or warning his owners about someone or something approaching. Baying is another word for howling. It is a distinctive, deep-chested sound. Bloodhounds for instance will *bay* naturally when they catch onto an interesting scent.

Chapter 11

Hand Cues – Pretty Handy!

Learn Special Hand Cues to Use with or Without Your Verbal Commands

Hand Cues. Why So Handy?

Here's why. You can use hand cues in addition to your verbal commands or separately. The handy part; say you're on your phone working from home while in an important conversation. You wouldn't want to say, *"Hold on, I need my dog to sit."* Instead, you could give the 'Sit' hand cue without verbalizing the command while continuing your discussion. *Pretty handy huh?*

"Sit" Hand Cue

To get your dog to sit on his hairy fanny, you want to hold up your hand up with your palm facing toward your dog. Similar to making the Stop sign.

Start training by having your dog sit down. Reward him with a click and a small treat. Now try this again and tell him to “Sit” while using the hand cue and click and treat. Practice this at least fifteen times. At this point, you are ready to try using the hand cue without a verbal command. Hold your hand up until he sits and then click and reward. You may have to make him sit with your hands to reaffirm the notion of what you are doing. Practice this at least fifteen times. Now change the context up a bit and begin practicing this in different locations, like the yard and out in public.

“Stay” Hand Cue

Holding your fist up may indicate power to we humans, but to your dog this will mean ‘Stay’. He should stop moving as soon as he sees this gesture and stay put exactly where is at. Curl your fingers into a fist and hold it up with your palm toward your dog.

Start training by giving your dog his 'Stay' verbal command. Reward him with a click and a small treat. Now try this again and tell him to "Stay" while using the hand cue and click and treat only when he stays in place. Practice this combination fifteen times. Each time a few seconds more in length. At this point, you are ready to try using the hand cue without a verbal command. Hold your fist up until he sits and stays, and then hold it for a few seconds and click and reward. Then practice this hand cue fifteen times and start to increase the Stay-time by small increments until he is able to stay in place for a full minute. Reward him when he does this without any verbal command. Now change the context up a bit and begin practicing this in different locations, like the yard and out in public.

"Down" Hand Cue

The down hand cue is self-explanatory because basically you are making a down motion from an outward flat position. Hold your hand in an outward position, with your natural bend, while your palm is facing the floor and make a lowering motion with your fingers and arm to a half-closed position. When successful your dog will immediately lie down when seeing this.

Start training by having your dog lay down with a verbal command. Reward him with a click and a small treat. Now try this again and tell him "Down" while using the hand cue and click and treat. Practice this at least fifteen times. At this point, you are ready to try using the hand cue without a verbal command. Hold your hand in this downward motion until he sits, then click and reward. You may have to make him lie down with your hands to reaffirm the notion of what you are doing. Practice fifteen times. Begin practicing this in different locations, like the yard and out in public. Reward when he follows the hand cue without needing a verbal command.

"Leave it" Hand Cue

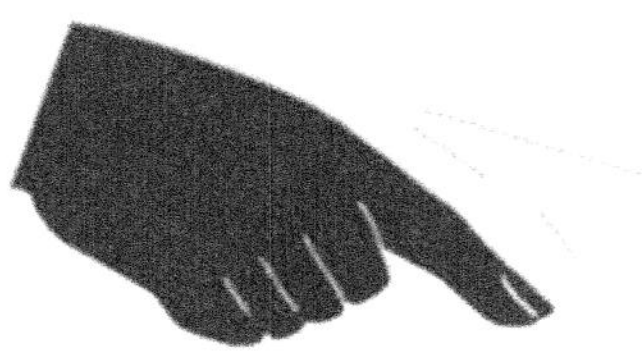

A semi toward and downward point with your index finger is how you command your dog to leave something alone or mind his own business. If he is starting to mess with food, an animal, a hole he likes to dig, your shoes, etc., you will use this point to let him know to leave well enough alone.

First train 'Leave it' with a verbal command when he messes with something he shouldn't. When he drops it, reward him with a click and a small treat. Next give him a toy or bone enjoys messing with, tell him "Leave it" while using the hand cue, click, treat when he obeys. Practice this command fifteen times. At this point, you are ready to try using the hand cue without a verbal command. Point until he leaves it, click and treat. You may have to make him leave it with your hands to reaffirm the action. Keep practicing this at least fifteen times. Change the context up and begin practicing this in different public locations. Reward when he follows the hand cue without needing a verbal command.

"Quiet" Hand Cue

Making the OK hand cue is a good way to tell your dog to hush when he is barking or braying. When he sees this signal, he will know to fall quiet.

Start training by having your dog quiet down with a verbal command. Reward him with a click and a small treat. Now try this again and tell him "Quiet" while using the hand cue, click and treat. Practice this command fifteen times.

Now you are ready to try using the hand cue without a verbal command. Hold the "OK" signal until he stops barking and then click and treat. Practice this at least fifteen times.

Change the context up a bit and begin practicing this in different locations, like the yard and out in public. Always reward when he does what you want and responds to the hand cue without needing a verbal command.

"Come" Hand Cue

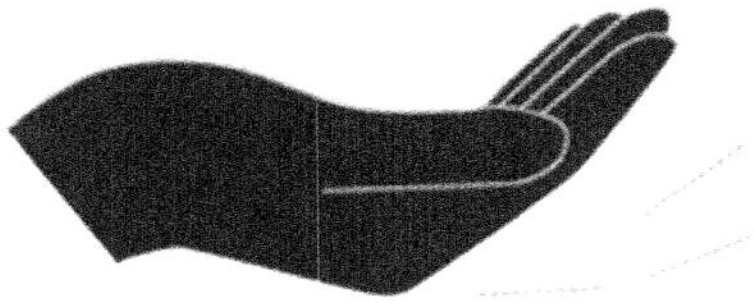

'Come' is formed by holding your hand palm up, with your fingers bent. Then wiggle your aligned fingers in a back and forth motion to let your dog know to approach you.

Start training by having your dog 'Come' with a verbal command. Reward him with a click and a small treat. Now try this again and tell him "Come" while using the hand cue and click and treat.

Practice this at least fifteen times. At this point, you are ready to try using the hand cue without a verbal command. Beckon to him with this hand signal until he comes and then click and reward. Keep practicing this at least fifteen times. Finally, change the context up a bit and begin practicing this in different locations, like the yard and out in public. Always reward when he does what you want and responds to the hand cue without needing a verbal command.

"Good Boy" Hand Cue

‘Good boy’ is simply a thumb’s up to show your dog that he is doing what you want. Rewarding him with this hand cue can be important to encourage him to continue the desired behavior. Start training by always giving your dog this hand signal when he obeys you or when he is being good but follow it up with verbal praise. Then move on to using it without verbal praise after a few times and give him a click and a treat whenever he obeys you. He will quickly learn to associate the thumbs up with being a good boy and getting a treat.

This concludes the primary hand cues you can teach your dog. We kept this section brief on purpose. To view and download even more helpful hand cues and information you can use for the best relationship with your dog, go to Newdogtimes.com.

Chapter 12

Alpha Dog

Learn to Understand Why Dogs Need an Alpha, and How You Can Be That Alpha.

Dogs are pack animals. This means they need a solid leader. You. Without your leadership, dogs can become a bit misguided. Therefore, you really want to become the alpha that your dog respects and looks up to. You want to become the alpha dog.

Understand that your dog instinctively craves your leadership. If you do not become pack leader as his alpha, he alone will assume the position. As a result, training goes out the window, leading to disobedient behavior, disastrous circumstance and non-domesticated decisions in actions. (*Such as tearing your new couch into a thousand pieces before breakfast).* Bottom line, you are to immediately establish alpha on day-one.

What is Alpha?

In a traditional dog pack, the alpha is the supreme leader. Basically, other dogs will respect him and do what he tells them to do in their unspoken language.

Alpha dogs are usually male; hence, if you have a female dog, you will have a bit more ease getting her to submit to you. But you can still make males submit without problems. This is because dogs are bred to coexist in harmony with humans and will submit to humans with gladness.

The thing is, your dog is looking for guidance. He needs a firm lead to get his head straight. No dog is truly a bad dog. But dogs without guidance are wild and can behave unruly. When you become the alpha, you become the leader your dog needs. You are able to give him commands and control his behavior. You can train him, and he actually listens to you. A good dog is a dog with solid leadership and guidance.

Your dog needs a single leader. Having multiple leaders will only confuse him. While everyone in your family can establish dominance over your dog and give him commands, just one person needs to be the true alpha who makes the executive decisions.

How do You Become the Alpha?

To become the alpha, you need to adopt the traits a dog will admire. Let's explore what these traits are:

- **Confident:** A calm demeanor, steady stance, decisive firmness, strong yet happy vocalizing depicts a confident alpha. Be confident in your commands and guidance while combining these other alpha traits and your dog will crave your leadership.

- **Firm:** Your dog is doing something you don't like so you tell him no and you don't let him get away with it. You don't tolerate bad behavior. When you give him commands, you speak in a tone that is firm and easy. Additionally, giving him commands, you make him mind and you refuse to allow him to ignore you. When you speak, you make him pay attention.

- **Unwavering:** You want to give your dog your undivided attention while working with him. You also want to be much focused. These two traits combined will help you get into your dog's mind and make it clear what you want from him. Give him your unwavering attention during training.

- **Clear:** You can't give your dog mixed signals and expect him to understand. He will get confused and let you down. If you want your dog to stay, don't beckon him to come to you. Be mindful of the signals you give him and tell him the one thing you want him to do. Give him very clear, specific signals.

- **Consistent:** You can't condone a behavior one day and then punish it the next and think your dog will understand. You must practice consistency. When your dog pees in the house, you must discipline him and show him what he did wrong in the same way each time. When he works hard or does a trick well, you must reward him the same way.

- **Intelligent:** You are the leader, which means you must be wise and show some wisdom and leadership. You must make intelligent decisions and show that you are smarter than your dog. This is the only way to lead the way and be alpha. So even if your dog tries to outsmart you, don't let him. Always have the dominant lead.

- **Fearless:** You should never hang back or be doubtful. Instead, you should want to take the lead without doubt, hesitation, or fear. You should be the one to lead when walking your dog and you should not let him shove you out of the way when you let him outside, no matter how big he is. You cannot let him jump on you, bark at you, or bite you. If he does something bad, you should discipline him. Tell him what to do without any fear and make him do it.

- **Dominant:** The more dominant you are, the more alpha you are. With your dog, you want to be top dog all the time. How does this look? It looks like you are not afraid to tell your dog no, and you tell him no and he listens. You perform dominance training and train him without feeling bad or letting him walk all over you. You have rules in the house that he must obey, and he does obey them because you have dominance over him. When you walk him, he walks proudly along at your heel and you reign him in when he tries to bind forward.

Adopt these traits and you can become the alpha person that your dog looks up to.

Becoming alpha is something that starts from the car ride home. You need to begin asserting your authority from day one. If you have an older dog, say a rescue, you can still begin the process. Even older dogs will seek a leader and look up to you if you present yourself as that leader.

From the first day, you can assert yourself as an alpha by potty training and showing your dog his crate and where he can go in the house. Let him know the rules from day one.

Start by showing your ultimate dominance. You want to walk straight and use firm movements around your new dog. You also want to make and hold eye contact. Do not act like you are afraid of your dog; use firm movements with him and avoid ever cowering away from him. Ignore him until you are ready to give him attention; do not let him command where you give your attention or when.

When he is not listening or is misbehaving, you can use a control technique to establish dominance over him: Grab hold of his muzzle (gently) and hold it until he submits. On top of this control, offer your dog love and praise to form a bond with him. Reward him when he is a good boy to show him that you are in charge and you control his behavior. And, of course, tell him no and put him in time-out when he misbehaves.

Be the disciplinarian. You decide when your dog needs to be quiet. You give the commands. You also feed him and set his schedule. One secret to bonding with your dog is to feed him by hand from his bowl and do not let him snatch food from you or growl at you. He must get used to you touching his resources and controlling them as you please. You can also cuddle with him but ensure that he only gets praise and love when he does something for you. Being too affectionate with your dog or giving him love when he demands it lets him know that he has control over you. That is a bad thing.

Above all, be number one. You are the first to eat and your dog must wait. You are the first to walk through doors and he must wait for you. While you walk him, you ensure that he walks behind you and lets you go first. Going first establishes your dominance and your dog will soon respect that.

Work on this each day and each moment with your dog. You must make sure that he is always your subordinate.

In the past, you have been timid with your dog. Maybe you stood back and let him rush through the door, or you flinched when feeding him table scraps for fear he would snap at you. Now you are the one to take the lead and make him mind. He is much more respectful, once you establish dominance and the alpha position. While it may seem "mean" or "unfair" to be dominant over your dog, really it is a wonderful thing because it enables you to give your dog the guidance, and he needs to create a harmonious living environment and relationship.

In Closing, I want to congratulate you on caring enough to learn how to adjust your behavior to improve your relationship with your dog. Things will be better now, and you can curb problem behaviors since your dog is under your alpha leadership.

Thank You!

Thank you *for taking the time to read this guide, and to train your dog.*

Because . . .

You Absolutely Rock!

(Just ask your dog :)

Chapter 13

Free - Gift for You

Please Accept My

Free Gifts

To You

Go To:

NewDogTimes.com

Legal Disclaimer:

The company publisher and its owners, officers, employees, contractors, and all participating or non-participant affiliates, along with the authors who have created this Bone Up Dog Training How To Book and Guide and its content resources, titled Bone Up Dog Training, by 'Karen Douglas Kane' and published by Craicom, is held harmless against any and all claims and allegations against it. Further the aforementioned parties will ever be in any conceivable strategy, effort, direct or creatively obscure way responsible at any time for the action of your pet, not now or in the future. Animals, without warning, may cause injury to humans and or other animals. Karen Douglas Kane, Craicom and all mentioned for the production and participation in creating the Bone up Dog Training Books, guides, Information, along with any and all outbound linked from or to resources are not in any way held accountable, or responsible for attacks, bites, mauling, or any other viciousness and or all other damages. We strongly recommend that you exercise caution for the safety of self, the animal, and around the animals while working with your dog. The company- publisher and its owners, officers, employees, contractors, and all participating or non-participant affiliates, along with the authors are not liable for any animal or human medical conditions or results obtained from training. While all attempts have been made to verify information provided in this publication, the company- publisher and its owners, officers, employees, contractors, and all participating or non-participant affiliates, along with the authors assume any responsibility for errors, omissions or contrary interpretation of the subject matter contained herein. The company publisher, authors and its owners, officers, employees, contractors, and all participating or non-participant affiliates, along with the authors assume no responsibility or liability whatsoever on the behalf of any purchaser or reader of the material provided. The owner of said dog training guide assumes any, and all risks associated with the methodology described inside the dog-training guidebook.

Thanks to Bill E!

Father, Leader, Winner, Example, Inspriation, Dog Lover

101

Printed in Great Britain
by Amazon

59829760R00060